US ELECTIONS RESULT 2021

Pedro Nicholas

Pedro Nicholas

CopyRight©2021 Pedro Nicholas

All Right Reserved

TABLE OF CONTENT

INTRODUCTION	3
CHAPTER ONE	5
STATE ELECTIONS: GUBERNATORIAL	5
CHAPTER TWO	13
A BAD OMEN FOR DEMOCRATS AND 4 OTHER ELECTION NIGHT TAKEAWAYS	13
CHAPTER THREE	17
CONCLUSION	17
2021 ELECTIONS: RESULTS AND IMPLICATIONS	17

INTRODUCTION

On Tuesday, November 2, 2021, the United States elections of 2021 were held in major part. The regular gubernatorial elections in New Jersey and Virginia were held during this off-year election. State legislative elections were also held in New Jersey and the Virginia Chamber of Delegates (the lower house of the Virginia General Assembly), as well as several state legislative special elections, citizen initiatives, mayoral races, and other local elections. Due to deaths or vacancies, two of the six special elections for the United States House of Representatives were held on November 2 or earlier. The first one took place on March 20.

Republican candidates earned substantial victories across the board in what has been dubbed a red wave election. In a major upset, Republican nominee Glenn Youngkin defeated Democratic nominee Terry McAuliffe in the Virginia gubernatorial race. On the first day of his administration, Youngkin promised to eliminate the teaching of critical race theory in public schools, oppose specific COVID-19 mandates and limits, and advocate for a low-tax, small-government agenda in Virginia. Within the Democratic Party, moderate nominees overwhelmingly defeated left-wing candidates, and progressive initiatives were mostly rejected; a proposal to defund and replace the Minneapolis police force was lost by a landslide.

The results were largely interpreted as a backlash against the Biden administration's social, racial and COVID-19 migration policies, as well as alleged economic interventionism, cultural liberalism, and wokeism within the Democratic Party.

CHAPTER ONE

State elections: Gubernatorial

In 2021, two states had regular gubernatorial elections, and one state held a recall election:

California: Governor Gavin Newsom, a Democrat, is facing a recall petition, primarily because of his handling of the COVID-19 outbreak. The recall election was set for September 14, 2021, by Lieutenant Governor Eleni Kounalakis, and voters began receiving postal ballots in August. The election focused on two issues: whether or not to recall Newsom, and who would take his position if he were to be recalled. The replacement ballot included a large number of candidates, including talk show host Larry Elder, financial analyst Kevin Paffrath, businessman John H. Cox, former San Diego mayor Kevin Faulconer, state assemblyman Kevin Kiley, media personality Caitlyn Jenner, and former U.S. Representative Doug Ose. Newsom was re-elected when the recall effort failed.

New Jersey Governor Phil Murphy, a Democrat, is seeking re-election for a second term. Jack Ciattarelli, a former state assemblyman, won the Republican primary. Gregg Mele was nominated by the Libertarian Party, Madelyn Hoffman was nominated by the Green Party, and Joanne Kuniansky was nominated by the Socialist Workers Party.

Virginia: Because the state's term limits prevent sitting governors from serving successive terms, incumbent Democrat Governor Ralph Northam will not be able to run for re-election until the 2025 gubernatorial election. Former Virginia governor Terry McAuliffe won the Democratic primary, while former Carlyle Group co-CEO Glenn Youngkin was chosen by the Republican Party. Princess Blanding, a Liberation Party candidate, also ran unsuccessfully in the election. The Republican Nominee Glenn Youngkin was anticipated to win the race by several media outlets, including DDHQ.

Gubernatorial lieutenant

In 2021, one state will hold a lieutenant governorship election: California.

Virginia: One-term Democratic Lieutenant Governor Justin Fairfax was eligible for re-election, but he chose to run for Governor instead. Former state delegate Winsome Sears was nominated at the Republican convention, and state delegate Hala Ayala won the Democratic primary. Sears won the election for lieutenant governor of Virginia on November 2, 2021.

Attorney General's Office

In 2021, one state will elect an attorney general:

Virginia has a two-term Democrat governor. Mark Herring, the Attorney General, ran for governor but withdrew to run for a third term. In the Democratic primary, he defeated state delegate Jay Jones. Jason Miyares, a state delegate, was nominated for the Republican nomination. On Election Day, it appeared that Miyares would defeat Herring and become Virginia's new attorney general.

Legislative

Elections for state legislatures in the United States in 2021 are the focus of this article.

Both houses of the New Jersey Legislature and the lower house of the Virginia General Assembly will hold elections. The New Jersey Senate and General Assembly are presently controlled by Democrats. The House of Delegates in Virginia is likewise controlled by Democrats, though only by a few seats, allowing Republicans a chance to retake power.

Mayoral elections are held on a local level.

In 2021, mayoral elections were conducted in a number of major American cities:

Burlington, Vermont: On March 2, three-term Democrat Miro Weinberger defeated Progressive Max Tracy in a tight re-election battle.

Springfield, Missouri: Ken McClure, a two-term independent, was re-elected on April 6 against Marcus Aton, an independent.

Tishaura Jones, a Democrat, narrowly defeated Cara Spencer, a Democrat, to succeed retiring one-term Democrat Lyda Krewson on April 6.

San Antonio, Texas: Ron Nirenberg, a two-term independent, won re-election against Greg Brockhouse on May 1.

On May 11, Republican Dave Bronson narrowly defeated Democrat Forrest Dunbar in a runoff for the position of acting mayor of Anchorage, Alaska.

Omaha, Nebraska: In a runoff election on May 11, two-term Republican Jean Stothert defeated Democrat RJ Neary.

US Election Results 2021

Arlington, Texas – On June 5, Jim Ross defeated Michael Glaspie in a runoff election to replace term-limited three-term incumbent Jeff Williams.

Mattie Parker defeated Deborah Peoples on June 5 in Fort Worth, Texas, to succeed retiring five-term Betsy Price.

Chokwe Antar Lumumba, a one-term Democrat, won re-election on June 8 against independents Les Tannehill and Charlotte Reeves.

Birmingham, Alabama: One-term Democrat Randall Woodfin defeated Democrats Lashunda Scales and William A. Bell to win re-election on August 24.

Mobile, Alabama: Two-term Republican Sandy Stimpson defeated Democrats Fred Richardson and Karlos Finley to win re-election on August 24.

Albuquerque, New Mexico: Tim Keller, a one-term Democrat, was re-elected on November 2 against Manuel Gonzales, the county sheriff and a fellow Democrat. Eddy Aragon, a Republican radio personality, came in third.

Boston, Massachusetts: Acting Democratic mayor Kim Janey, who took over after Marty Walsh resigned to become United States Secretary of Labor, lost her bid for re-election to a full term in the primary. Michelle Wu, the previous president of the City Council, defeated Annissa Essaibi George on November 2.

Due to term restrictions, two-term Democrat John Cranley is ineligible to run for re-election. Former mayor David S. Mann was defeated by Hamilton County Clerk of Courts Aftab Pureval.

Frank G. Jackson, a four-term Democrat, has declared that he would not seek re-election. Justin Bibb, a nonprofit executive, defeated Kevin J. Kelley, the president of the City Council, to take his seat.

Detroit, Michigan: On November 2, two-term Democrat Mike Duggan defeated former deputy mayor Anthony Adams, who was also a Democrat, to win re-election.

US Election Results 2021

On November 2, one-term Republican Francis X. Suarez defeated businessman Max Martinez in a resounding re-election victory in Miami, Florida.

Due to term restrictions, two-term Democrat Bill de Blasio was unable to run for re-election. Curtis Sliwa, the founder of the Guardian Angels, was beaten by the Democratic nominee, Brooklyn president Eric Adams.

Wade Kapszukiewicz, a one-term Democrat, defeated independent former mayor Carty Finkbeiner on November 2.

Those who are eligible for the position

New York, Albany: Kathy Sheehan, a two-term Democrat, is seeking re-election.

Justin Wilson, a one-term Democrat, is standing for re-election in Alexandria, Virginia.

Marty Small Sr., a one-term Democrat from Atlantic City, New Jersey, is running for re-election.

Byron Brown, a four-term Democrat, is running as a write-in candidate after losing the Democratic nomination to India Walton, the former executive director of the Fruit Belt Community Land Trust.

Ravinder Bhalla is a one-term Democrat from Hoboken, New Jersey.

Steven Fulop is a two-term Democrat from Jersey City, New Jersey.

Andy Schor, a one-term Democrat, is standing for re-election in Lansing, Michigan.

Danene Sorace, a one-term Democrat, is standing for re-election in Lancaster, Pennsylvania.

Joyce Craig, a two-term Democrat, is seeking re-election in Manchester, New Hampshire.

Jacob Frey, a one-term Democrat, is standing for re-election in Minneapolis, Minnesota.

LaToya Cantrell, a one-term Democrat, is campaigning for re-election in New Orleans.

Ben Walsh, a one-term independent, is running for re-election in Syracuse, New York.

Incumbents who are ineligible or who are retiring

Ray O'Connell, a one-term Democrat, was defeated by Matt Tuerk for re-election in Allentown, Pennsylvania.

Keisha Lance Bottoms, a one-term Democrat in Atlanta, has declared that she would not seek re-election.

Stephen K. Benjamin, the three-term mayor of Columbia, South Carolina, has declared that he will not seek re-election.

Harrisburg, Pennsylvania will hold a mayoral election in 2021. Eric Papenfuse, the city's two-term incumbent mayor and a Democrat, sought for a third term, but was defeated by City Council President Wanda Williams. Papenfuse stated on

September 15, 2021 that he would pursue a write-in candidacy in the November General Election. Williams defeated Papenfuse in the general election by a margin of more than 2–1.

Bill Peduto, a two-term Democrat, was defeated for re-election by state representative Ed Gainey.

Lovely Warren, a two-term Democrat, was defeated by at-large city councilor Malik Evans for re-election in Rochester, New York.

Jenny Durkan, a one-term Democrat in Seattle, has declared that she would not seek re-election.

Rick Kriseman, a two-term Democrat from St. Petersburg, is ineligible to run owing to term limitations.

Nan Whaley, a two-term Democrat from Dayton, is running for Governor of Ohio instead of re-election.

Elections in tribes

Several significant Native American tribes, including the Aroostook Band of Micmacs, Citizen Potawatomi Nation, Confederated Tribes of Siletz Indians, and Mashpee Wampanoag Tribe, will conduct tribal executive elections in 2021.

On June 5, the Cherokee Nation will hold elections for its Tribal Council.

In a special election in July 2021, St. Regis Mohawk Tribe people elected Ronald LaFrance Jr. as chief, succeeding incumbent chief Eric Thompson. In the normal June election, Thompson narrowly defeated LaFrance, who ran as a write-in candidate, but the victory was called into question by appeals, culminating in the special election.

CHAPTER TWO

A bad omen for Democrats and 4 other election night takeaways

Glenn Youngkin, a Republican, won the governor's election in Virginia, defeating Terry McAuliffe. In an even bigger shock, Republican Jack Ciatarelli came within a percentage point of incumbent Democratic Gov. Phil Murphy in New Jersey.

The New Jersey election could go to a recount, but the fact that it was so close indicates how much energy Republicans had going into Tuesday night. Both of these outcomes are shocking to a Democratic political elite that has had little positive news in recent months.

The delta variation and prices have risen throughout that time, the US exit from Afghanistan has been tumultuous, and the Democrats' agenda on Capitol Hill has been blocked. While the economy has improved and coronavirus infections have decreased, we are still a long way from President Biden's summer of liberty.

All of this has resulted in a drop in Biden's poll ratings and political capital. The cherry on top is that in the 2020 presidential election, Democrats lost a state that Biden won by ten percentage points and were nearly deadlocked in a state that Biden won by sixteen.

Here are five key lessons from Tuesday's results:

It's not a good sign for Democrats' chances in 2022.

It's only one night, and you don't want to read too much into the outcomes.

That was especially true of Virginia, which had gotten so much attention because, except from New Jersey, it was effectively the only game in town.

Because the Virginia election is one of the first opportunities for opponents of the sitting president to express their displeasure, history is on the side of the party not in power in the White House. New Jersey has a history of defying the odds; since 1977, no Democratic governor has been re-elected in the state.

And McAuliffe had his own issues as a candidate (I don't believe parents should choose what schools should teach.

But this one is self-evident.

Since 2009, Democrats have won every statewide election in Virginia and the last four presidential elections, including Biden's double-digit victory. Despite the fact that the race in New Jersey had appeared to be tightening in recent days, Murphy remained the overwhelming favorite.

Democrats were already facing an uphill battle to keep control of the House in next year's midterm elections, and this result isn't likely to boost their spirits. Is it possible that more Democrats in Congress may resign and leave? Keep an eye out for that.

The suburbs are still battlegrounds.

The suburbs moved toward Democrats throughout Donald Trump's presidency. They took control of the House in 2018, for example, owing to victories in center-right districts.

As a result, many people assumed that college-educated suburbanites would always vote for Democrats.

However, Tuesday night's results in both states revealed that this is not the case. Youngkin and Ciatarelli were able to outperform Trump in numerous suburban regions in 2020, as well as outperforming Trump in several rural counties.

Pedro Nicholas

It's a wake-up call for Democrats and a blueprint for other Republicans to follow, with image and education as critical factors.

Republicans could have found a way to campaign in the post-Trump age.

Youngkin went for a non-offensive suburban dad and businessman look, complete with a fleece vest and a smile. He didn't appear onstage with Trump, but he did touch on some of the same problems that Trump supporters are concerned about. (In one commercial, he claimed that the FBI is attempting to quiet parents.)

While Youngkin was on Fox News promoting talking points that pleased the right, he was also running ads around the state that highlighted a softer side. Youngkin did everything he could to avoid appearing or sounding like Trump while remaining loyal to his base and accepting the former president's endorsement.

Democrats attempted to portray Youngkin as a Trump clone, but it appears that Virginia voters did not buy it. Even in a Democratic-leaning state, connecting a Republican to Trump only gets you so far in this campaign.

The fact that the Trump/conservative base could be mobilized even without Trump on the ballot — and with turnout that topped 2017 turnout in both states — was also crucial.

On education and racism, Democrats require a response.

Whether you call it a racist dog whistle, as McAuliffe did, or white grievance, Democrats must come up with a compelling response to the (often inaccurate) allegations about how children are taught about systemic racism in schools.

Wherever you look, it appears like the college-educated, suburban white voters that Democrats thought were breaking their way have united around 'Critical Race Theory,' according to Democratic pollster Cornell Belcher on MSNBC on Tuesday night.

CHAPTER THREE

Conclusion

2021 elections: Results and implications

Both parties are looking to the first big elections of the Biden era to establish voter preferences and devise winning strategies for the future. In New Jersey and Virginia, statewide and local elections will be the focus of this year's elections. The latter has grown increasingly important in recent weeks, as polls show Republican Todd Youngkin and former Democratic Governor Terry McAuliffe in a close battle.

The 2021 off-year elections have historically provided valuable information into voter sentiment, especially as the 2022 midterm elections approach. Democrats' victories in 2017 forecasted the 'blue wave' of 2018, much as Republicans' clean sweep in 2009 projected success in 2010. Continued COVID safety policies, economic anxiety about inflation, structural racism, and other issues will likely be top of mind for voters. In a post-Trump election, how would Democrats fare? Can Republicans profit from Biden's dwindling popularity? Will this year's polls be accurate?

The Brookings Institution's Governance Studies program will offer a webinar on November 8 to discuss the results of the 2021 off-year elections and what they signify for both the Democratic and Republican Parties—as well as the Biden Administration's agenda. Voter turnout, election management, and repercussions for the 2022 elections will be discussed by the panelists...

www.ingramcontent.com/pod-product-compliance
Lightning Source LLC
Chambersburg PA
CBHW050330220526
45465CB00005B/2208